GOD'S LIGHT WITHIN

CHARLES T. ROSS, JR.

This book is dedicated to Scott A. Pojack.

He is my brother in all, without whom nothing in my life would be possible.

One man, moments from death in an emergency room, was visited by an Angel that spared his life, spiritually awakened him and then sent him on a journey to find God. This is his story...

God's Light Within

By Charles T. Ross Jr.

ACKNOWLEDGMENTS

My undying gratitude and many, many thanks are owed by me to so many for making this book possible.

Sue Walker: A true friend and spiritual guide who has been with me many millennia.

Heather Forbes: A very successful and published author whose advice helped make this book a possibility.

Sergey Forbes: A genius who is responsible for the formatting of my words into a book. A true friend.

Chester Pojack: A pillar of his community and success in all he has done. He was responsible for proofing my manuscript.

Wendy Kopp and Patti Goodwin: Dear and treasured friends whose love and support helped me in this enormous task.

CONTENTS

.

PREFACE

So, I was born, I lived, and now I'm dead.

What's it all mean?

Why was I born?

Why did I live?

Why did I live when and where I did? What about the choices that I made in my lifetime, and why?

Am I ready to be held accountable for every action and thought I have ever had in my lifetime?

Now that I have crossed beyond human life and am sitting before God himself, as he waits to hear my first words, what will I say?

Wait...

Before I could say anything, my entire life, from the moment of my first breath to the last gasp of air I drew into my lungs, flashed through the memory of my very soul.

I was now simultaneously conscious of every single thought, word spoken or unspoken, and action or inaction that I ever took.

No matter how good I thought that I might have been in life before my death, is it even possible to stand before my very Creator and not be ashamed now that I know that He knows everything I do?

My prior thoughts and/or beliefs about religion, atheism, Christ, Mohamed, David, or anything else now mean nothing. I am sitting before God himself and now know without question that he is definitely real, making denial no longer possible in any way.

In the most immeasurable least bit of the fastest moment within a moment and in the most perfect clarity, I finally understood that I am a part of the One that is God and that nothing in creation, including myself, is ever apart from God.

I, the being that I now am, have had every barrier of ignorance, racism, hate, and anger removed from within me.

Sitting before God himself, I now had experienced the Mt. Everest of epiphanies. I realized that even though I possess the memories of the entire life I just lived, it is void of every single emotion I had ever experienced, except for one, love.

As this epiphany now grows and becomes my new reality, I realize that my soul is not new, and I have added to the very purpose of it, which was to gain more knowledge and experience in the never-ending quest for complete wisdom within God and the absolute perfection that his love is.

Why am I telling you this? The answer is simple. I experienced it, and so have you. The only difference between you and me is that I remember it and have been given the opportunity to share it with you.

I have skipped ahead and just told you the ending. However, the ending is only the beginning, and this is the beginning of my story.

∾

MY AWAKENING

*I*n my research, I have read and been told that some people who have survived a major trauma or near-death experience (N.D.E.) are spiritually awakened. By "awakened," I mean that they become aware of what some people consider to be psychic gifts. I am now a believer.

I don't refer to these as gifts or as being psychic. It is merely the ability to tap into your higher consciousness or your connection to the Divine, which is much more aware of things that your other senses can't detect. It is, in actuality, not a gift but a realization or the ability to remember a mere fraction of the capabilities and power of your true self, your immortal soul.

My awakening process first began in January of 2001 when I developed a headache. This was no ordinary headache. It was horrendous. This headache wouldn't go away and kept building in intensity for a couple of days. It got to the point that I couldn't eat or drink. I couldn't even move without becoming so nauseated that it caused me to vomit. The worst part was the pain. Pain that most people could not even imagine, and I wouldn't wish upon anyone.

I am not female, so I am unable to compare it with the pain that women must feel during labor. I can tell you, though, that it was so bad that I wished I were dead. I have even told people since that day that I would rather be kicked in the crotch every five minutes for a whole week than go through that pain again.

Fortunately for me, Scott was taking care of me while I was sick. He came into my bedroom to check on me and found me lying on the floor in the fetal position, crying. The last time he had checked, I was just lying in my bed. I'm sure he was quite shocked to find me on the floor like that. I don't even remember how it was that I ended up on the floor.

I said, "Scott, I need to go to the emergency room because I think that I'm dying." At the time, I was 34, with the macho/tough guy personality that wouldn't allow me to even go to a doctor, let alone an emergency room. You know, the whole walk it off or rub dirt on it thing. (Thankfully, I have since come to realize just how stupid that kind of attitude is.) Knowing me as well as anyone could, Scott didn't even question my wanting to go. He and my mother helped me get into the car, and we drove to the hospital.

I lived in the southern Denver metro area, so they took me to Littleton Hospital. After being triaged, I was immediately taken into the emergency department without waiting. I was in so much pain that I could barely speak. I was given ample pain medication, which had absolutely no effect on reducing the pain. I remember requesting more pain medication and being told that if I were given more, I would probably overdose and die. I told them that I didn't care. I would rather be dead.

The doctors, not having any clear idea as to what was causing me so much pain, ordered an immediate CAT scan of my brain.

After reviewing those test results, a doctor came into my room and said that they had found something in my head. I was told that I had a blood clot in my Sagittal Sinus Vein and that I would need to be admitted to the hospital right away and started on a treatment of intravenous blood thinners to hopefully eliminate the blood clot.

Being told I had this clot in my Sagittal Sinus Vein, I had assumed that it had something to do with my sinus cavity and that I simply had some kind of sinus infection that caused a little clot. Not a big deal.

WRONG!

However, in my defense, I wasn't exactly thinking all that clearly at that moment, nor had I received any education on the different brain parts other than a very basic understanding I had learned from biology class in school many years prior. How many people who have not gone to medical school would know what the Sagittal Sinus Vein is?

I was moved to a room in the intensive care unit (I.C.U.). Even though being placed in the I.C.U. should have been a huge clue to me, I didn't realize how very serious my condition was until a different doctor came into my room a couple of hours later.

The very first thing this new doctor said to me was that he couldn't believe that I was still alive. If compassion or even a decent "bedside manner" were a requirement to be a doctor, this guy would be doing something else for a living.

I was quite surprised. I didn't even know who this guy was. For a minute, I thought he was probably in the wrong room.

Most likely because I was staring at him like a deer caught in headlights, he introduced himself as the hospital's on-call neurologist. He then explained to me that the Sagittal Sinus Vein is the main vein in your brain that separates the two halves or hemispheres of your brain.

We had some discussion, and it was my limited understanding that I would be treated with blood thinners in the hopes that the clot would dissipate on its own.

After spending about a week in the hospital being intravenously pumped full of Heparin (a blood thinner) and Dilaudid (a synthetic morphine that is about 100x more powerful than Morphine itself), I was sent home from the hospital with prescriptions for multiple blood-thinning pills and painkillers. I was very weak but feeling better with a level of pain that was made bearable with the painkillers. I was very happy to be alive and at home. Anyone who has spent any time as a patient in a hospital would probably agree with me that there is a lot of joy in just leaving the hospital.

Three weeks later, on Valentine's Day, I was lying on the couch watching television, still trying to recover from my experience. Suddenly and very unexpectedly, the real nightmare began. My right leg began to tingle like that falling asleep feeling you get in your limbs now and then. I didn't think much of it. However, after the tingling was over, my leg fell asleep and I couldn't wake it up. The very same thing then happened to my right arm.

I had no idea what was happening to me, but I knew it wasn't a good thing. Luckily, my mother was there helping out and watching over me as I recovered. I called for her and asked her to call my doctor and see if they knew what was going on with me.

While she was on the phone with my doctor's office, the same thing happened to my face and my tongue. It was as if someone had sliced me exactly in half. My right side was completely paralyzed! I was confused and very scared. I had no idea what was happening to me.

Within moments, I then lost the ability to talk. Not just because my tongue was half-paralyzed, but also because my brain was screwing up. I could hear and understand what others were saying to me, but when I tried to say something, the words just seemed to get lost somewhere between my brain and my mouth, resulting in just grunts and weird sounds coming out of my mouth instead of words. It was the most bizarre and truly horrifying experience of my life.

As my symptoms worsened, my mother gave up trying to get information from my doctor's office and hung up the phone. She and Scott loaded me into the car and rushed me back to Littleton Hospital. Upon arrival, Scott ran and got a wheelchair, loaded me into it like a sack of potatoes, and rushed me into the emergency room as fast as he could.

I remember the triage nurse asking me questions and me trying to answer her. I must have looked and sounded like a severely mentally handicapped person to her. She asked my mother if I always spoke and acted like that. My mother, not usually one to lose her cool or curse, became very upset with her and yelled some very colorful language at her, basically telling her that she was an idiot and that is why we are here, because it was not a normal condition for me to be in. (Duh! Why would we be in the emergency room if this was normal for me?)

After being in the emergency room for a few minutes, I found out that I was having what the hospital calls an MVA and others refer to as a stroke.

I had, of course, heard of strokes, but I really didn't know what one was or even the symptoms or signs of one. I also had thought that strokes were something that only elderly people should worry about. I didn't even know that having a blood clot in my head that I should be concerned about having a stroke. I was much more naive than I ever thought I could have been.

Another CAT scan was performed. The scan showed that even though I had been on multiple types of blood thinners for about a month, my blood clot grew four times larger than it had been on the day that I was released from the hospital, and was now causing me to have a stroke because it was interrupting the blood flow of my brain.

I was told that my condition was beyond the ability of the hospital to deal with. You can probably imagine how much more horrified I felt when I was told that this hospital wasn't qualified or able to treat what was wrong with me. I was told that I would need to be airlifted to Swedish Hospital, which had a level one trauma center and was equipped to deal with my particular situation.

I was informed that I would need immediate surgery to remove the clot. I was also told that the surgery I was in dire need of had an over 90% mortality rate, which means I would most likely not survive the operation.

If I chose not to have the surgery, I would continue to have multiple strokes until I died. Not really much of a choice, I could either go for the less than 10% chance of surviving the operation that would most likely kill me, or just stay where I was and have a 100% chance of dying.

My logic was that I really didn't want to have the surgery because I thought that it was pretty pointless.

Obviously, because I am writing this and you are reading it, you know that I chose to have the operation. However, until this very moment, I have never told anyone why I really chose to go through with the operation.

I chose the operation not because it gave me the slightest chance of living, but because if I didn't, my family would have stood beside the hospital bed and watched me die in front of them. I did not want to put them through that experience. So I made that choice for them, to let them have at least some hope for me, but mostly to relieve them of the horror of witnessing my death.

Adding to the reality of my situation, the emergency room staff at Littleton Hospital handed me a cordless phone and told me to call everyone that I wanted to and say goodbye. Let me tell you, that's about as real as it gets.

While waiting for the helicopter to arrive with my mother and Scott at my side, helping me make the phone calls to loved ones, a priest came into the room.

I remember this incident very vividly, but if it were not for my family members being in the room who witnessed this priest, I would have later thought I dreamed it.

As soon as I saw the priest approaching my bedside on my right side (the paralyzed side), I instantly felt a sense of calm and peace wash over me. It was an experience that I cannot even put into words. I was no longer scared or even worried about death. I was kind of in a state of bliss, for lack of a better word.

The priest laid his hand on my right arm, and we had a short conversation. It didn't occur to me right at that moment, but I could feel his very warm hand resting upon my arm.

A feeling I should not have had, seeing as that arm was completely paralyzed. It also didn't occur to me that I could speak to him able to answer his questions until later.

I don't think the priest was in the room for more than three minutes, if even that long. I remember after we briefly spoke, he briskly walked to the door, opened it, and walked out of the room without saying a word to anyone else in the room.

Scott wanted to speak with the priest privately, so he followed him out of the room.

The door had a hinge that was designed to close on its own. The door immediately closed behind the priest, and Scott arrived at the door within mere seconds of it closing, opened it to walk out and join the priest.

The door opened into a "T" hallway. Upon leaving my room, you would need to walk quite a distance to the right or left before you could reach another door or hallway. Scott looked in both directions and could not see the priest anywhere. He was instantly shocked and confused as to how he could have disappeared so quickly. It wasn't possible.

Scott immediately went to the nurse's station to inquire about the priest they had sent in and where he could find him. He was told that the hospital did not have a priest, they had not sent a priest into the room, and they had not seen a priest. Soon afterwards, the Flight for Life helicopter arrived, and I was loaded into it and flown to Swedish Hospital, where they were going to go into a vein in my thigh and travel up to my brain to bust that clot. It was a type of angioplasty surgery, except it was in my brain.

After about an 8-hour surgery, I woke up. I could move. I was no longer paralyzed, and I could speak. It was truly a miracle. I should have been dead, let alone recovered.

That was no priest. It was an Angel, an actual, real Angel of God, hidden within the flesh costume of a priest. With a seemingly simple touch from that Angel, my life was spared.

For a long time after that day, I suffered from survivor's guilt. I was thankful to that Angel for saving me and giving me a second chance at life. However, I also thought, who am I to be given such a chance? What great thing(s) in life am I supposed to accomplish to be worthy of such a gift?

Since that Angel touched me, I have just known things. Things that I did not previously know or even could have known. For instance, whenever I hear someone talking about Heaven, Angels, creation, or anything along those lines, I just know if what they are saying is right or not. It wasn't a memory, just a knowing. Like facts stored in me, I can't explain it better than that.

Being physically touched by that Angel not only saved me but left an imprint of knowledge within me. Being touched by one of God's most holy creations, one of His Angels, was like being touched by Heaven itself.

I also developed a deep intuition. I can usually tell if someone is lying to me and if someone is a bad person or not. I can always tell when I am near a person who has been praying a lot because I can feel it and even see a glow to them that others don't have.

I didn't think much more of these newfound abilities until recently. In 2015, they just seemed to explode, increasing exponentially. I even felt like I doubled my IQ. Some things that I had no comprehension or understanding of now seemed so simplistic to me.

I understood many of Leonardo da Vinci's deepest mysteries that he left behind for us. (A story for another day.)

I was able to physically and mentally see much, much more. Things that I never could have imagined even existed. I had thought that figuring out da Vinci would be the biggest thing I could ever hope to accomplish in my life. In actuality, he merely provided the key that opened a door to unlimited information available to us. Da Vinci provided me with the tools that I needed to begin the greatest investigation and realizations of my life.

With the increase in my awareness, now I can also see people's energy and the energies from any object you can think of, from a rock or a blade of grass to the moon.

I had never put much thought or belief into metaphysical things. Now it had consumed my every moment.

I sought out the services of a very gifted person who had a much better understanding of these types of awareness and control of them to help me understand and comprehend what I was dealing with.

I found one local to me, Suiking Lloyd. A woman that I researched and really believed in and knew wasn't a scammer just wanting money. She turned out to be a miracle to me and a gift to the entire world. She is absolutely amazing and told me things about myself she could not have possibly known, which removed any skepticism I may have had about her.

Without even asking, she told me about the priest who came to me that day in the hospital when I was dying from a stroke. She confirmed that, as my family and I had suspected, it was not a priest but an Angel that visited me. She also told me that it wasn't an ordinary Angel; it was the Archangel Gabriel that visited me.

An Archangel of God took the physical form of a human male dressed as a priest and laid his hand upon me, breathing life back into my body and leaving me with a Divine imprint. I was indeed very humbled, to say the least.

She and I had a lengthy conversation, including my purpose in life. I have learned that everyone has a specific purpose. The very meaning of life is not a difficult question to ponder at all. The meaning of life is simply to gain knowledge and experience to grow your soul.

I feel that I was very fortunate to discover my main purpose in life and why I was spared from bodily death. My main purpose is to decipher messages and share them. Those messages will mostly be delivered in the form of books. I know that I will be writing at least twelve books. These books, with this being the first, will explain the Divine side of life and the role it plays in our lives. Future books will go into deeper detail, revealing the Divine truths about different subjects that will be revealed to me and shared with you when the timing is right.

Originally, I had a lot of concerns about the purpose given to me. My first concern was, of course, that people would think that I am insane. Another concern was how people would react to the information that I bring them, and would do more harm than good. Her answer to me about these inquiries and concerns that I had was like a sharp slap in the face.

The Angels told her to inform me that it was not my place to decide what messages to give or to whom. They would make sure that whoever needed to see or hear the messages would, then perceive whatever meaning is meant for him/her. My job is just to give the information, and they would worry about everything else.

She also told me that I would be doing this for 30 years. I was told this on the day of a Blood Moon, which by no coincidence is only seen once every 30 years.

I have had several conversations with her since then, and she has helped me to not only come to terms with this great task laid out before me, but also how to gain understanding and some control of this new awareness and the awesome opportunity and responsibility that was granted to me. I now feel very blessed and humbled rather than burdened.

I have come to realize that being aware of my purpose is a relief, knowing what I should be doing with my life rather than stumbling through it blindly. I will also share that it's an incredible feeling to live by knowledge rather than by faith. I get to go through the rest of my life truly knowing that there is a God, a Heaven, Angels, an eternal afterlife, and eternal bliss. I have no reason to ever fear death.

I will begin with two separate experiences that happened to me involving strangers that further convinced me of just how special this knowledge granted to me is.

I always enjoy going to this particular park near my home because it is filled with many things that I find very beautiful. There is a wonderful little pond that is home to many Canadian Geese. The entire park has a very 'being in the woods' feeling to it, with many trees and wildlife such as squirrels, rabbits, and the like. On my first visit after receiving the Divine Imprint, many squirrels walked behind me, following me around the park.

I felt like Dr. Doolittle. (I have found that animals have a constant awareness of the Divine. I can only assume that they sensed the recent Divine 'smell' on me and were attracted to it.)

On this visit, during my walk, I noticed a woman and a couple of children sitting at one of the tables in the park. Upon seeing her, I couldn't help but feel sad for some reason. As moments passed, a thought kept running through my head.

The thought was that this woman had been praying a lot and was asking for a sign from God. I thought to myself that I am no sign of God, and if I say anything to this woman, she will think I'm nuts.

The thought persisted; I couldn't get it out of my head. It was like someone was punching this thought into my head with a nail gun. I knew if I didn't speak to this woman, the thought would not stop; it was merciless.

It was obvious to me that I didn't have a choice. I had to speak to this woman.

So, gathering up all the courage I could, I approached this woman, this stranger to me, and I said, "Hi, I know you don't know me, and this is going to sound crazy, but I feel that you have been praying a lot and are waiting for a sign from God. I was told to tell you that he has heard your prayers, and I am that sign for you. You will be OK. "

Upon completing that sentence, the woman burst into tears. She told me that she had recently become homeless and had been praying all day. She thanked me profusely.

I was so shocked by her reaction, I think I was only kind of half-hearing her because I was so numb, just like when the adrenaline rush is over and you have that feeling of all the blood rushing out of your legs, making you all wobbly. I had expected to be slapped, yelled at, anything but this. To this day, I don't know which one of us was more surprised by the brief conversation that we had.

Although I have been back to that park on numerous occasions, I have not seen her again. I felt terrible that I couldn't do more to help her with her situation when we met that day, other than to just offer her words.

Later, when I was thinking about her and wishing her well, even though she didn't tell me, I felt (another knowing within me) that she had become homeless not due to a financial reason, but an abusive situation that she mustered the courage to walk away from for the safety of herself and her children. I have the "knowing" that she is doing much better and is now safe and much happier because of her courage to make a very difficult but needed change. I was merely a vessel used by the Angels to deliver a message that gave her that final little push that she needed. I am humbled to have been a part of that Heavenly help.

The second experience that was calling out to me for assistance was about a week later.

I was driving to my doctor's office to pick up a prescription. While driving there, I kept seeing the image of an elderly man wearing a light brown British racing cap. I knew that I would be talking to this man. I figured he would probably be sitting in my doctor's office when I got there.

When I arrived at my doctor's office, the door was locked, and a sign on the door said that they were closed for lunch. I didn't know they were closed for lunch. Two things went through my head: one was that it was a twenty-minute drive from my home, so I didn't want to do the drive again, and I would need to find something to do for an hour. The second thought was that obviously, this guy that I saw in my head wasn't in the office. I was actually kind of relieved, thinking I just avoided some possible embarrassment.

With the woman in the park, I did not perceive any images, only a thought. Having the image of the man was different from my first experience; it was much more powerful, yet no less confusing.

To kill time, I decided I would go to the mall across the street and eat lunch in their food court to wait until my doctor's office opens. While driving to the mall, I saw the 50's diner in the same parking lot as the office and thought that sounded good and would be easier, as I wouldn't have to mess with leaving the parking lot and all the traffic lights, etc.

I went to the 50's diner and sat at the counter, and ordered a hamburger. After I was there for a few minutes, the very guy that I had envisioned in my head walked into the diner and was seated at the table right behind where I was seated at the counter.

I instantly recognized him. I almost freaked and passed out right there. If I had any blood in my legs, I probably would have gotten up and run out of there. Instead, I sat there eating my burger, occasionally glancing over my shoulder at the man sitting with a woman whom I assumed to be his wife.

I knew I was going to have to speak with him, but I wasn't looking forward to it. I was thinking to myself, "What am I supposed to tell this man"? As soon as I asked myself that question, an answer just popped into my head.

I was suddenly aware of the fact that this man was going through a very severe health crisis with either himself or a family member, and that he had been praying a lot. Again with the praying a lot. I don't know what the exact crisis was, but I just seemed to know of the problem's existence, just like I know my own name.

I decided to finish my burger and pay the check before speaking with him. I thought if I embarrass myself or cause a scene, at least I would be able to immediately walk out the door. I ate as slowly as I could, but finished my burger, and the man was still there.

I walked over to the man's table and put my hand on his shoulder, and told him that the Angels have heard his prayers, and I was supposed to tell him that he was not alone in dealing with his situation.

The man was speechless, but his wife, with tears forming in her eyes, thanked me and told me that they had been praying a lot. I didn't feel it was needed for me to stay and say or discuss anything further with them, so I left and immediately felt a wave of calm and peace come over me. It was an awesome feeling that words can't describe.

Later, while reflecting on this episode, I was amazed at the realization of all the things that had to come together to put that man and me in the same place at the same moment. I know that I left drained of my energy and very tired. Upon coming home from both of them, I took a nap.

Although I have been able to sense people who have been praying heavily or suffering from some kind of life crisis when I encounter them by walking or even driving by them, I have not felt "Angelically compelled" to speak with anyone else as of yet. So, I haven't.

Honestly, not being compelled, I have lacked the courage to just walk up to those I know who could use some words of encouragement. I am now ashamed of putting myself with my childish fears of embarrassment above those that I might be able to help with just a few simple words.

As I sit here at my desk writing this, I have pledged to the Angels that I will no longer do that. If I suffer some embarrassment or someone thinks I am a freak, so be it. I will get over it.

I very specifically remember attending a Christmas Eve church service. This, incidentally, was the first time (and last) I had been in a church service since the realization of the gifts granted to me.

The energies and spiritual images that I saw in that church that night were amazing and nothing short of a miracle to me. However, I was also very disgusted by other things that I saw and felt. For example, the priest giving the sermon was an elderly man whom I believe was not in the greatest of health. What bothered me about him was that I just seemed to know that he was (at that time) suffering from doubt in his faith and beliefs, and was more concerned and fearful about his pending death than anything else. I was shocked and disgusted by this, yet I pitied him at the same time. Here I was looking at and listening to a man give a Christmas service who had dedicated the majority of his life to his faith in God, and he didn't even believe what he was saying himself. I thought that this man, of all people, should not fear death, knowing that there is so much beyond the death of our bodies. I saw this man for the hypocrite that he was.

I also realized just how scripted and robotic this service was. All the prayers, what the priest was to say, what the congregation was to say in response, songs...everything that was to be said was scripted just like a play or movie. The meaninglessness of it all hit me like a ton of bricks and made me feel nauseous. I realized that it serves no one, especially God, to just recite words with no feeling.

I began to wonder if this congregation had become so used to just saying these same words and sentences over and over again if it even had any meaning to them anymore.

I think that having faith and belief in God is very necessary and a very good thing. I also think that when you speak to God, you should choose words from your own heart that mean something to you. If words you are merely reading from a program or book don't resonate with you, why are you saying them?

The last thing that the Angels absolutely insisted that I do was to prepare myself about a month before that church service, and it was to quit smoking. It's not like an Angel appeared before me and said, "I want you to quit smoking." I just knew that they had wanted it. I am supposed to be bringing messages for 30 years. I think continuing to smoke would not be conducive to my lasting for the 30 years.

Obviously, quitting smoking is hard. I was doing well; I was down to only a few cigarettes a day. One day, I was down to my last cigarette on hand, and I said to the Angels, "O.K., this is it, this will be my last cigarette."

It wasn't my last cigarette, though. I was weak and gave in to the cravings and got hold of some more cigarettes. I knew it was wrong. I felt like a little kid sneaking a cigarette or something. That night, I was taken to the emergency room yet again.

I thought that I had a blood clot in one of my lungs as my chest hurt very badly, and previously, having had this problem, I knew what it felt like to have a blood clot in one of my lungs.

It turns out that I did not have a blood clot. One of my lungs had completely collapsed.

When the Doctor showed me the X-ray, it reminded me of the classic Yin/Yang symbol; one lung appeared solid white on the X-ray, and the other solid black. In medical terms, they call a collapsed lung a pneumothorax.

The fact that my lung collapsed without injury or a coughing fit, etc., is called a spontaneous pneumothorax. I had never personally heard of this. I have heard of collapsed lungs from people being shot, in car accidents, and things like that, but never spontaneously.

I also found that I do not fit the profile of a person who it is likely to happen to, which is mostly younger, tall, and skinny people. I am none of those things.

I didn't mention what I thought to the Doctor because I didn't think the timing was right and didn't want a mental evaluation added to his list of treatments for me, but I knew what caused it. The Angels were unhappy with me for not keeping my word to them. I told them that I had my last cigarette, and then I had another one. They crushed my lung to teach me a lesson.

I spent a week in the hospital and learned my lesson well. Quite simply, when the Angels ask you to do something, YOU DO IT! Also, don't ever break your word to them.

They demonstrated their power to me very well; first when they spared my life from my stroke, and then again when they crushed my lung. They have ways of convincing even the most hardheaded, stubborn people such as myself. After all, they know you better than you know yourself. They know your soul.

I have always had a love and feeling of awe for God's most holy creations, the Angels. I also now have a newfound respect for them, like a parent.

I know that they protect you, want the best for you, and, although a very rare circumstance, will punish you if needed to teach you important lessons. Think of them as "Heavenly parents" watching over billions and billions of God's children like you and me.

∼

GOD, ANGELS AND THE
UNIVERSE

❦

IN LAYMAN'S TERMS

*A*s previously discussed, I was initially very confused by the things, sights, and visions I was having, which prompted my initial visit to Siuking Lloyd.

For those who are skeptical that Angels and even anything beyond human life exist, I understand that. I was there once, but was fortunately awakened to the Divine.

It is my sincere hope that with the beginning of the messages that I am going to present in this first book, all skepticism will cease to exist. This hope is not pure fantasy, as I am going to uniquely do something that no one else has ever done. I am going to present these messages that I am receiving from the Angels in a simple and non-religion-based format so that all will be able to interpret and understand. All will be able to see with their own eyes and feel with their soul that there is indeed Divinity and that we need to respect it.

We are in what I call "The Time of Discovery." This is the time when science and metaphysics will begin to come together to complement one another and make sense of the universe, as they should have admitted to long ago.

Before I start presenting these messages, I want all to have an understanding of our Creator and the Universe. I feel that this information is paramount to your understanding and interpretation of the messages that I am to deliver.

Know that I refer to our Creator, the Creator of ALL that exists, He who has neither beginning nor end, as God. God has at least 72 different names that he has been referred to since the creation of humans, and other names known by the Angels that aren't even able to be pronounced by the human tongue. Depending upon your religion and/or beliefs, you may call him by a different name. What you choose to think of as His name makes no difference as to who He is. I have even simplified our Creator by referring to Him as "He." God has no defining gender. He is all, He is everything.

Know that I do not consider myself to be a prophet or even anyone special and want no one to think of me as such. I am merely one soul, here living on earth in this body to do a specific job, as we all are. I am very honored and humbled to have been chosen to work with the Angels so closely. Know that many souls are living among us that have similar purposes. Those souls are now being referred to as the "Chosen Ones."

I am not religious. I am 100% spiritual. Let me explain the difference. Religion is following one group or person(s) view or interpretation of God and how to worship him and conduct their lives. Being spiritual is believing in God without boundaries.

Being spiritual is knowing that God is 100% forgiveness and unconditional love. Spiritualists don't need commandments and/or written rules to tell them that you should not commit murder, cheat on your spouse, steal, etc., and to know what is right and wrong in living their life. They are naturally good souls and treat everyone and everything with love and respect.

If one were to break down all the religions that worship a divine creator, one would find that most have the same general beliefs and sometimes even the same historical accounts of events. They just have different ways of practicing their beliefs.

There is nothing wrong with true religion in my opinion; it just isn't for me. I think that some people really need it and that it can provide a very strong sense of family and community for its members. There is most definitely nothing wrong with uniting and helping one another for good causes.

My biggest problem with religion is what's NOT being told. For example, the King James Version of the Holy Bible was written by a group formed by the king, who decided what would and wouldn't go into the Bible. It was meant as a tool to help keep people in check for the king's rule. I am not saying that there is no truth in the Bible. I am saying that I believe that some parts have been omitted and others changed at the whim of the compilers. The Dead Sea Scrolls continue to prove this more and more all the time.

The Holy Bible has very little detail to offer about the life of the Holy Mother Mary or even the Life of Jesus before his last couple of years before He was crucified.

From the time that Christ was born, it was no secret as to who he was. The Bible does speak of the guiding star and those who journeyed to witness his birth, and then goes blank for about 30 years.

You should ask yourself why it is that the entire life of the Son of God would not be worth discussing in the Holy Bible? Why was the decision made not to include this information? Would it possibly have a bad reflection on the prominent religion at the time?

The Holy Mother Mary was dropped off at a church when she was about 3 days old, where she was raised and hand-fed by Angels. She was groomed to be as pure as humanly possible from the time of her birth in preparation to give birth to the Son of God.

Within a few hours of his birth, Christ was speaking. As Mary, Joseph, and Christ traveled, they were always followed by crowds of people. After Christ was bathed, people would jump into the water that bathed his body and were instantly healed of their illnesses, wounds, or diseases. At the age of just six months, as Mary, Joseph, and Jesus travelled, they ran into a group of thieves that had control over the area they were travelling through. Christ spoke with the two thieves who would be hanging on crosses to his left and right when he would be crucified about 30 years later. He told them of this future for them, and his party was granted safe passage through the territory. I guess being told of their future by a six-month-old baby captured their attention.

I, like everyone, should have a huge problem with the Vatican. The Vatican has a library/archive that is filled with tremendous knowledge that you will most likely never see. I believe it to be against God to not share that knowledge, or any knowledge, with the world. If I were Catholic, I would be demanding that the entire world be given complete access to the archives.

What are they hiding from their own worshippers and the entire world? Even more importantly, why?

The most profound and telling part of the Holy Bible is one of the first sentences, where it says in Genesis, "**God said, let there be light.**" The word "light" has a much deeper and profound meaning to God and us than the Bible goes into. All life, including our own souls, is made up of God's light and energy.

All souls were created at the same time in pairs, hence soul twins; one male and one female soul were created together. There are no "old" or "new" souls. Our souls are immortal.

Our souls continuously seek growth. Growth is the way our souls become closer to God. The soul requires knowledge and experience to grow in God's light. A soul is able to gain knowledge and experience in many different ways. Living a human life, with all of its experiences, is a very effective way of growing your soul with love, knowledge, and experience.

Many have heard of the aura or colors that surround each person's body. (Science has now proved this existence.) These colors/lights are created by the energy of your soul within. People who have tapped into their higher or Divine consciousness can see these without the aid of specialized cameras or computers. The soul has its own glow to it that is independent of the human aura. Souls within human flesh have three very distinct colors to them. White, grey, and black. A white soul is one with God. A black soul is not in line with God and must gain much knowledge and growth to be aligned with God. A grey soul is a step up from a black one, but still has a long way to go to be aligned with God.

To begin to understand immortality, you must understand that time does not exist. Time is nothing more than a simple word. Time is a concept that people have created so that the human brain can comprehend events and place things in order so that they make sense to the human brain. In reality, there is no past, present, or future; it is just the now.

Once you accept this seemingly complicated concept, you will find that it is a very simple one, and you will begin to tap into your higher consciousness, revealing knowledge and senses you didn't realize that you had all along. (Buddhists and others like them have realized this for thousands of years.)

The Universe is not infinite. It is finite, but is one of an infinite number of universes. This is referred to as the "Multiverse Theory." Ask yourself, how is it possible for astrophysics to hypothesize that the universe is getting smaller or bigger? How can you say that something that has no end is getting bigger or smaller?

The sciences have just begun to realize that much more exists than what we are able to see, such as dark matter. Science also knows that our universe spins on its own axis. You must ask, What does it spin around? A question that science is ignoring.

There are an infinite number of universes or dimensions (I consider them the same) on top of one another and intersecting one another in an infinite number of places and ways. When a universe/dimension intersects another, it creates what science calls a black hole. A black hole is the gateway to another dimension or universe, which is why light or nothing else returns from one. It doesn't disappear; it just goes to where we cannot yet see. (I will get into this topic much more in detail at a later date, as it is a whole book in itself.)

We, along with EVERYTHING, exist at God's will. We are because He thinks it, and it is. See it for what it is; everything in creation exists in God's mind. Therefore, God is ALL of us and ALL in creation. Which also makes us a part of God. That means that all that we make or create is also created by God. Even if we were to find that the human race was actually "engineered" by another race, that does not mean that God didn't create the Human race.

It would just mean that God created us using something else he created; it really doesn't make a difference. We are, because God wanted it.

I have often heard people ask or wonder why such bad things like tragedies, accidents, and illness/disease, etc. happen or exist if there is a God. The answer to that is simple.

As I previously stated, we are living life to experience and gain knowledge to grow our immortal souls. There are some lessons, such as compassion, that only God can teach.

Everything in God's creation has a purpose. Everything in God's creation has a polar opposite. It would not be possible for us to experience great happiness if sadness didn't exist. How could we experience great love without great loss? We could not know what great truth or goodness is without corruption and great evil.

A very important part of, and reason for, our existence is to experience things for God. As we are all a part of God, he feels and knows all that we do. He lives and experiences "life" through us. Think about that for a minute. If ten people were to witness an accident, you would hear ten different stories about that event. Each person sees it differently, interprets the event differently, experiences different emotions, etc. God simultaneously collects all of those different aspects of the same thing from each of us. Multiply that by ALL that exists in every universe/dimension, and you will understand a mere fraction of what God is and his greatness.

To think of God as anything other than 100% untainted and unconditional love is not only ridiculous but disgusting.

To begin to start understanding God, look to one seemingly simple gift that He gave to us. Dogs. A dog naturally possesses those same very basic qualities that we use to define God.

A dog lives its life displaying unconditional love, loyalty, and forgiveness to us. A dog naturally lives life the way all of mankind should strive for and hope to achieve.

Could you imagine how peaceful this world would be if we were able to achieve what dogs are born with?

Beyond us and other life, God created His angels. Angels were God's first creation. Like the electrical impulses of our brains carrying out our thoughts, turning them into movements, etc., think of Angels like God's electrical impulses that carry out his thoughts. Unlike us, Angels are perfection and carry out God's will instantly and perfectly. They, like God, are complete love and compassion. However, we were given a gift that God did not even grant to his Angels: free will.

Although Angels can certainly think and act upon their own, they are limited to actions within God's will. To better understand an Angel's limitation of interference in our lives, think of them like a police officer in the U.S. A police officer has certain regulations, policies and laws they must follow. However, they also have the authority in some cases to not ticket or arrest someone when they think it would be beneficial to that individual and society. Thinking in that sense, you can understand why Angels do and can step into and interfere with a person's destiny to help them.

Due to the fact that we have free will, we can often make the wrong choice. We all have Angels assigned to us to watch over us and help us. An Angel will generally not inject themselves into our lives without us asking for their assistance. What we call "intuition" is our Angels trying to guide us in the right direction or in making the right decision. The feeling of "deja vu" is your soul's way of telling you that you are on the right path to fulfilling your purpose and life lessons.

You can have your Angels help you at any time with any matter you wish. All you have to do is ask them for it. The only requirement is belief, honesty, and sincerity with them.

God is no different than any other parent in that he wants us, his children, to be happy and have all of the best of everything.

The most important part of life that the Angels want us all to understand is that without experiencing any challenges, hardships, losses, disappointments, etc., what could you possibly gain? What would the point of living be if you were to just sail through life with no challenges or obstacles? There would be nothing gained or experiences added to grow your soul. To go a little further, I will tell you that you have already picked or decided most things that you will go through or experience during your lifetime. Before you chose a life, you decided what kinds of things you wanted to experience to grow your soul. This is referred to as your life contract.

Before you chose to be born into a human life, you chose what you wanted to experience during this life to grow your soul. Nothing but love, knowledge, and experience can grow your soul. All of those tragedies that you experience throughout your life are already decided upon by your soul. Before being born, you decided that you needed to learn about something for whatever reason your soul needed the knowledge and experience of. I know we all think at times that we have more going on than we can handle. In reality, we don't. You may have chosen a very difficult life because you lived previously and experienced very little of what you really needed to. In some cases, your main life purpose may be to serve the needs of another or all of us.

If you are not serving your life purpose, you will know it. You won't succeed, and you won't be happy. You will never be happy or feel right until you are following your path.

Yes, we do divert from our primary purpose to address things that arise, which need to be experienced and can only be gained at that time.

You will always be guided back to your path; all you need to do is listen to your intuition. Your Father, our God, will not steer you wrong. Just listen and you will hear him.

There is a hierarchy to the Angels. The highest level of Angels is known as Archangels. Seven is such an important Heavenly number.

There are 7 Archangels
There are 7 Heavens
There are 7 Worlds
There are 7 Days of the Week
The Angelic Alphabet is based on 3 families of 7 letters
There are coincidentally 7 holes in the human head: 2 eyes, 2 ears, 2 nostrils, and the mouth.

The 7 ArchAngels each have 12 Realms to divide and part. The 12 Realms are what Astrology is based upon.
Each Realm has 777 Cities.
Each City has 60 Castles
Each Castle has 60 Towns

The eldest and most powerful Archangel is Michael. Michael is God's first creation and His right hand. Michael, like God and the other Archangels, is Omnipresent. That means that they have the ability to be in multiple places or ALL places simultaneously.

There is a vast discrepancy in opinion on how many Archangels there are and the classes and orders of the Angelic realm.

I will delve into much more detail about the different kinds of Angels in a book dedicated to just them.

Just know that Angels do exist and that they are very much a part of your life. The Angels are always with you to guide and protect. The Archangel Michael is my Guardian Angel and guide. Gabriele is the Archangel who visited me in the hospital.

Angels are a very important part of my life that I depend upon every day. Angels are just as big in your life; you just may not realize it yet.

∼

THE AKASHA

One of God's other dimensions or universes is called the Akasha. Some call it the Akashic Records or the Hall of Records or even the Book of Life. Call it by any name you wish, for it is the same. The Akasha is very complex. Although I mean no disrespect or injustice to it, I am attempting to put it into its most basic form to make it somewhat understandable to all.

In this dimension, all records are stored. When I say all records, I quite literally mean ALL. Every thought, word, deed, emotion, invention, etc., ever in any dimension or universe that ever was or will be is held as a permanent record in this dimension. Think of it as the universal supercomputer with every conceivable piece of data stored in it without end.

Many have accessed parts of these records. For example, there is a written account of the world's most famous psychic, Edgar Cayce, doing that very thing. People such as Leonardo da Vinci, Albert Einstein, Nikola Tesla, the Sumerians, Egyptians, Mayans, etc., just to name a few, were able to tap into parts of this dimension for knowledge. Many theoretical physicists even believe that this plane of knowledge exists.

Every soul has its own Akashic Record. Nobody, regardless of his or her abilities, can tap into or "hack" your Akashic record without your permission or for an evil purpose.

When you speak to a person able to tap into their higher consciousness to speak with people that have crossed over, such as a medium like Theresa Caputo or Tyler Henry, or Matt Frazer, to name a few, they are tapping into Akashic Records via spirits guiding them and allowing them to access and interpret the information. These spirits or guides can be souls assigned to this task, or even Angels or the very Guardian Angels whose job is to protect and guide you.

All "psychic" phenomena of every kind originate from this same dimension. The only difference is in what specific knowledge is being tapped into.

For further, deeper understanding of this very complex subject, there are probably thousands of books on the subject, as well as numerous Internet resources on the subject that you can research.

There are those among us with the very noticeable gift of tapping into this Hall of Knowledge in one or more ways. Everyone should know that people can achieve some level of these gifts on their own. It takes patience, study, and belief in yourself and that of the beyond. If you don't believe that you can do it, you never will.

If you want to find out more about yourself and your purpose, future, connect with loved ones that have crossed over, past lives, etc., there are a multiplicity of ways to do this on your own. I would personally start your research on the Internet and go from there.

For those who want the same knowledge but do not have the time or patience to learn to do this on their own, it is not hard to find someone to do it for you, generally for a charge.

I would, however, be very wary of paying anyone who uses nothing other than some type of oracle deck to do a reading for you.

I say this simply because you could purchase those same cards yourself, read the instructions included with them, and give yourself your reading with no prior training. If this interests you, I would recommend any of the oracle decks by Doreen Virtue. Doreen is very connected to the Angels, and her cards are designed not to allow negativity or darkness into your readings. The same can't be said for the traditional Tarot deck or an Ouija board. I would not even allow an Ouija board in my house or on my property. I don't dabble with anything that could allow darkness near me. I also recommend that you stay away from "magic." All magic taps into dark energies; you don't need or want that in your life.

At first, I was kind of really put off by the idea of people making money by charging people for such a gift given to them. However, I eventually realized that this world operates on money and everyone needs a way to support themselves and their family, so I came to accept that realization. I do feel, though, that it is a sin not to share Divine knowledge in some way.

I would never dream of charging money or accepting any payment from anyone that I was compelled to deliver a message to, such as the two incidents I mentioned in my awakening period.

Although I have a few gifts granted to me, the most special and prized one by me is sight. I mentioned earlier that I could see energies, auras, souls, and the like.

The moon phases have a great impact on me, and I find full moons absolutely amazing. To me, staring at the moon is like watching a drive-in movie. I see what looks like movies playing on the screen that is the moon. What I did not mention earlier is that seeing into the Akashic Records is my biggest, strongest, and clearest gift.

Operating within the Akasha itself is my gift and where my life purpose lies. It is where I have and will receive everything that I will be showing you. That is why I refer to myself as a Universal Librarian. Everywhere I look, I find Akashic Records stored. So, to me, it is like being a librarian with complete access to the library. All I need to do to get information is to take a book off the shelf and open it up, and take a look.

The best way that I can explain what I see is that I can see through the veil, for lack of a better term. I am able to see multiple dimensions at once. For example, when I look at a tree, I can see that same tree in countless dimensions. That same tree in our dimension looks very different in other dimensions. It takes on different shapes, has different things engraved in it. It provides a different set of information or records for each dimension. In some dimensions, I can see thousands of faces in trees.

I see most clearly from elemental items. Trees work for me. However, so do granite, concrete, cliff walls, minerals, water, fire, etc. The most amazing and clear images and information come through to me from crystals.

I find the fact that I get my best information from crystals slightly amusing. That reason is that the next big leap in computer storage technology uses crystals. That technology is called Quantum Storage. Computer geniuses are currently trying to figure out how to store data on crystals.

One has successfully found a way to store some very limited data in the form of light already. It is believed that a very thin layer of quartz crystal, I'm talking the thickness of a human hair, would be capable of storing billions of terabytes of information. With that being said, it would stand to reason that with just a few ordinary-sized full crystals, we would be capable of storing every piece of computer data that we humans have ever collected.

That isn't that hard to believe once you realize that most people's cell phones carry more computer technology than the Apollo 11 that we landed on the moon.

The best and most unique part of my gift of seeing into the Akasha is the fact that I can share a lot of what I see with you. I have found a way of combining the energy of my gift with the technology of computer-enhanced imagery to show you a lot of what I can already see. Please note that when I say "computer-enhanced", know that I am not adding anything to these pictures I will be showing to you. I have only adjusted the way that what is already there is viewed. (Occasionally, I may circle an object within a picture or something similar; however, that will be made quite obvious, and I will mention that I have done so.)

This ability will answer many age-old questions while at the same time provide you with a whole new set of questions that you never even thought of asking before.

You will see things that you never knew were possible or existed. I will merely show you the images and messages, but will, for the most part, leave the interpretation of them up to you as an individual. I believe that each piece of information will have a different meaning for each person, and I will not dictate what it should mean to you. My next book will be devoted to images that I have found within crystals.

~

GOSPEL OF THOMAS (TRANSLATED BY THOMAS O. LAMBDIN)

⚜

INTERPRETATION BY CHARLES THOMAS ROSS, JR.

I have interpreted the Gospel of St. Thomas as translated by Thomas O. Lambdin, which was found among the Dead Sea Scrolls. This Gospel is the words of Jesus Christ himself and was never included as part of the Holy Bible.

The words that were spoken by Jesus Christ are in shaded boxes. My interpretation of his words is directly below the shaded boxes (layman's terms).

Gospel of Thomas (Translated by Thomas O. Lambdin)

These are the secret sayings which the living Jesus spoke and which Didymos Judas Thomas wrote down.

(1)

> And he said, "Whoever finds the interpretation of these sayings will not experience death."

If you find the truth within the words of Christ written herein, you have found Heaven and Eternal life.

(2) Jesus said,

> "Let him who seeks continue seeking until he finds. When he finds, he will become troubled. When he becomes troubled, he will be astonished, and he will rule over the All."

This matches perfectly with how truly spiritual individuals are currently "becoming." Once a person has awoken to the light, they first feel empty because life almost seems pointless, and they are filled with an emptiness now knowing that living is very limited. Once you get past that, you start to evolve your spirit to the point where the mind, body, and spirit become one.

At that point, you become one with the Universe, God, everything. You become part of the connection that we and everything are.

(3) Jesus said,

> "If those who lead you say to you, 'See, the kingdom is in the sky,' then the birds of the sky will precede you. If they say to you, 'It is in the sea,' then the fish will precede you. Rather, the kingdom is inside of you, and it is outside of you. When you come to know yourselves, then you will become known, and you will realize that it is you who are the sons of the living father. But if you will not know yourselves, you dwell in poverty and it is you who are that poverty."

If you believe that Heaven is an actual place, then you are lost. If you think Heaven is above you, then birds of the sky are smarter than you. If you think that Heaven is in the Ocean, then the fish are smarter than you are.

You are already a part of Heaven. Heaven is within you and outside of your body. Your spirit is already one with all. When you realize that, then you have found the light, or Heaven, and you will be able to experience it.

(4) Jesus said,

> "The man old in days will not hesitate to ask a small child seven days old about the place of life, and he will live. For many who are first will become last, and they will become one and the same."

A person who is elder and has lived many years realizes that a newborn child is fresh from Heaven. The realization comes that we are all from the One, God, and are all one. A newborn has left the light to experience life as the elder is right now. One day, the elder will return to the light, as the newborn child will also do.

(5) Jesus said,

> "Recognize what is in your sight, and that which is hidden from you will become plain to you. For there is nothing hidden which will not become manifest."

To those who have not awakened to the spiritual side, the light and knowledge are hidden from them. Once you realize that you are part of the one, you will begin to see all that is currently hidden from you, and then nothing will be out of your reach.

(6) His disciples questioned him and said to him,

> "Do you want us to fast? How shall we pray? Shall we give alms? What diet shall we observe?"

Jesus said, "Do not tell lies, and do not do what you hate, for all things are plain in the sight of heaven. For nothing hidden will not become manifest, and nothing covered will remain without being uncovered."

The disciples were basically asking Jesus how we as people should worship God. How should we eat? Should we fast? Should we make sacrifices? Jesus answered them by saying Live life simply. Don't lie, don't do things that you don't like to do. Nothing is hidden from Heaven, and Heaven hides nothing from you. Once you find the light within yourselves, you will see and know all.

(7) Jesus said,

> "Blessed is the lion which becomes man when consumed by man; and cursed is the man whom the lion consumes, and the lion becomes man."

Jesus is referring to the light, or Heaven, as a lion. Blessed is the man who sees Heaven and becomes one within it. Cursed is the man who lives separate from Heaven.

CHARLES T. ROSS, JR.

(8) And he said,

> "The man is like a wise fisherman who cast his
> net into the sea and drew it up from the sea full
> of small fish. Among them the wise fisherman
> found a fine large fish. He threw all the small
> fish back into the sea and chose the large fish
> without difficulty. Whoever has ears to hear, let
> him hear."

Jesus is telling everyone to listen to him, "Whoever has ears to hear, let him hear." He is referring to Heaven or the light as a big fish. A wise man will see many little things, or meaningless things in his life, ignore those things, and choose the big thing which is the light.

(9) Jesus said,

> "Now the sower went out, took a handful (of
> seeds), and scattered them. Some fell on the
> road; the birds came and gathered them up.
> Others fell on the rock, did not take root in the
> soil, and did not produce ears. And others fell
> on thorns; they choked the seed(s) and worms
> ate them. And others fell on the good soil and it
> produced good fruit: it bore sixty per measure
> and a hundred and twenty per measure."

Jesus is referring to God as a sower who threw seeds upon the ground. We are the seeds. Only some have taken root, and those that have are producing endless fruit.

(10) Jesus said,

> "I have cast fire upon the world, and see, I am
> guarding it until it blazes."

42

Jesus is referring to knowledge as "fire." He is guarding the knowledge until it is realized.

(11) Jesus said,

> "This heaven will pass away, and the one above it will pass away. The dead are not alive, and the living will not die. In the days when you consumed what is dead, you made it what is alive. When you come to dwell in the light, what will you do? On the day when you were one you became two. But when you become two, what will you do?"

Jesus is saying that Earth is Heaven or an extension thereof. It will pass away, or merge as one with the all. Before you were born into life, you were one with the light. When you were born, you became two: a body with the light or spirit within the body, making two. What will you do with life to grow your soul when you are living as two?

(12) The disciples said to Jesus,

> "We know that you will depart from us. Who is to be our leader?"

> Jesus said to them, "Wherever you are, you are to go to James the righteous, for whose sake heaven and earth came into being."

The apostles are asking Jesus who they are to follow after Jesus is crucified. Jesus tells them to follow the apostle James, who is righteous wherever he may be. James was a devout and true follower of Jesus during his time of life on Earth and was the second apostle to die after Jesus. Jesus proclaims that the reason God created man was for the sake of James and people like him.

(13) Jesus said to his disciples,

"Compare me to someone and tell me whom I
am like."

> Simon, Peter said to him, "You are like a
> righteous angel." Matthew said to him, "You are
> like a wise philosopher." Thomas said to him,
> "Master, my mouth is wholly incapable of
> saying whom you are like."

Jesus said, "I am not your master. Because you
have drunk, you have become intoxicated from
the bubbling spring which I have measured
out."

> And he took him and withdrew and told him
> three things. When Thomas returned to his
> companions, they asked him, "What did Jesus
> say to you?"

> Thomas said to them, "If I tell you one of the
> things which he told me, you will pick up stones
> and throw them at me; a fire will come out of
> the stones and burn you up."

Jesus asked his disciples to compare him to someone they knew.
Thomas, the one with the wisest answer, told him that he is
comparable to no person that he has ever met. Jesus told him
that he is not his master, as God is.

He then took Thomas away from the others and instilled three
items of knowledge upon him that are not revealed to anyone
else. Thomas, when asked what he was told, could not put
anything into words and could only say that the knowledge
given to him would destroy them. Thomas was wiser and in
tune with his spiritual side at that point than the other apostles
who were present. The other apostles were not ready to hear
the knowledge that Thomas was given.

Thomas, at a later point, then wrote this Gospel, where the knowledge given to him by Jesus is most likely included.

(14) Jesus said to them,

> "If you fast, you will give rise to sin for yourselves; and if you pray, you will be condemned; and if you give alms, you will do harm to your spirits. When you go into any land and walk about in the districts, if they receive you, eat what they will set before you, and heal the sick among them. For what goes into your mouth will not defile you, but that which issues from your mouth - it is that which will defile you."

Fasting was a religious practice. Jesus is saying that following a religion can lead to sin. Praying can cause you to be condemned by those of other religions.

If you give alms or sacrifices, you will harm your soul, as God does not desire sacrifice in his name. Jesus also says, as you visit foreign places, listen to what they say, as that can not harm you. What can harm you is what you say. To heal the sick among them is to instill knowledge in them.

(15) Jesus said,

> "When you see one who was not born of woman, prostrate yourselves on your faces and worship him. That one is your father."

Jesus is simply saying that if any person is born into the human race by anything other than a human female, that is God and to worship him. Even Jesus was born to a human mother, Mary.

(16) Jesus said,

> "Men think, perhaps, that it is peace which I
> have come to cast upon the world. They do not
> know that it is dissension which I have come to
> cast upon the earth: fire, sword, and war. For
> there will be five in a house: three will be
> against two, and two against three, the father
> against the son, and the son against the father.
> And they will stand solitary."

The mission of Jesus was not to bring planetary peace. He came to bring us the wisdom of God and his Heaven. His gift was knowledge, which is the key to eternal life.

After Jesus came, many wars and conflicts in his name and still go on to this day. Stay true to yourself and the word of God.

(17) Jesus said,

> "I shall give you what no eye has seen and
> what no ear has heard and what no hand has
> touched and what has never occurred to the
> human mind."

Heaven, the Light, the Other Side, is that which no human eye has seen, what no ear has heard, and no hand has touched. The other side is only accessible through the spirit, not of the body. This is the truth and knowledge from Jesus.

(18) The disciples said to Jesus,

"Tell us how our end will be."

Jesus said, "Have you discovered, then, the
beginning that you look for the end? For where
the beginning is, there will the end be. Blessed
is he who will take his place in the beginning;
he will know the end and will not experience
death."

The spirit or soul is eternal. The soul has no death. God has no
beginning or end. The beginning is God. Blessed is the soul that
sits with God for eternity.

(19) Jesus said,

"Blessed is he who came into being before he
came into being. If you become my disciples
and listen to my words, these stones will
minister to you. For there are five trees for you
in Paradise which remain undisturbed summer
and winter and whose leaves do not fall.
Whoever becomes acquainted with them will
not experience death."

Jesus is describing awakening to your spiritual side while in life.
Blessed is the one who comes into the knowledge of light before
he dies and is reborn into it. If you become a disciple of the
teachings of Jesus, you will realize that there is no death, only
the continuation of your spirit in the one who is God.

(20) The disciples said to Jesus,

"Tell us what the kingdom of heaven is like."

He said to them, "It is like a mustard seed. It is
the smallest of all seeds. But when it falls on
tilled soil, it produces a great plant and
becomes a shelter for birds of the sky."

When asked what Heaven is like by his disciples, Jesus says it is
like a small mustard seed when planted in the right soil becomes
a shelter. Tilled soil is a metaphor for the light of a soul. When
Heaven hits the soul, it finds 'tilled soil' and Heaven becomes its
shelter.

(21) Mary said to Jesus,

"Whom are your disciples like?"

He said, "They are like children who have
settled in a field which is not theirs. When the
owners of the field come, they will say, 'Let us
have back our field.' They (will) undress in their
presence in order to let them have back their
field and to give it back to them. Therefore I
say, if the owner of a house knows that the thief
is coming, he will begin his vigil before he
comes and will not let him dig through into his
house of his domain to carry away his goods.

You, then, be on your guard against the world.
Arm yourselves with great strength lest the
robbers find a way to come to you, for the
difficulty which you expect will (surely)
materialize. Let there be among you a man of
understanding. When the grain ripened, he
came quickly with his sickle in his hand and
reaped it. Whoever has ears to hear, let him
hear."

"They are like children in a field which is not theirs." Jesus is saying that people who are not familiar with spiritual knowledge are like innocent children who are uneducated. The "thieves" that will come to rob you are the ones that bear false prophecies and mistruths designed to lead you astray. If you are prepared and armed with the knowledge and truth of the light that is God, you will be the victor and win every battle.

(22)

Jesus saw infants being suckled.

He said to his disciples, "These infants being suckled are like those who enter the kingdom."

They said to him, "Shall we then, as children, enter the kingdom?"

Jesus said to them, "When you make the two one, and when you make the inside like the outside and the outside like the inside, and the above like the below, and when you make the male and the female one and the same, so that the male not be male nor the female; and when you fashion eyes in the place of an eye, and a hand in place of a hand, and a foot in place of a foot, and a likeness in place of a likeness; then will you enter the kingdom."

Jesus is again referring to the light that is your soul. Humans are souls born into flesh. The two, the body and the soul. When you make the two into one (awakening to the spiritual side and knowledge of God), you realize that all is truly one within God. That is the kingdom of Heaven.

(23) Jesus said,

> "I shall choose you, one out of a thousand, and
> two out of ten thousand, and they shall stand
> as a single one."

Jesus again refers to the All as one. When you are once again in your light or spirit form, you will be merged within the one. Numbers are meaningless. Billions of souls will all be as one.

(24) His disciples said to him,

> "Show us the place where you are, since it is
> necessary for us to seek it."
>
> He said to them, "Whoever has ears, let him
> hear. There is light within a man of light, and he
> lights up the whole world. If he does not shine,
> he is darkness."

Jesus is telling his disciples that the light of Heaven is already within you. Once you find the truth of knowledge, your body will light from within that others will see, not with their eyes but with their third eye, or soul. Those who have not yet discovered the truth remain dark.

(25) Jesus said,

> "Love your brother like your soul, guard him like
> the pupil of your eye."

Jesus is explaining that your brother, or one that has found the knowledge of light, should be guarded, because he is you, you are he. Again, we are all one.

(26) Jesus said,

> "You see the mote in your brother's eye, but
> you do not see the beam in your own eye.
> When you cast the beam out of your own eye,
> then you will see clearly to cast the mote from
> your brother's eye."

The mote or speckle or gleam of light in your brother's eye comes from the light of the soul within. You will be unable to see the light in another's eye until you find your light within yourself.

(27)

> "If you do not fast as regards the world, you will
> not find the kingdom. If you do not observe the
> Sabbath as a Sabbath, you will not see the
> father."

If you cannot find the truth of God, you will not find God.

(28) Jesus said,

> "I took my place in the midst of the world, and I
> appeared to them in flesh. I found all of them
> intoxicated; I found none of them thirsty. And
> my soul became afflicted for the sons of men,
> because they are blind in their hearts and do
> not have sight; for empty they came into the
> world, and empty too they seek to leave the
> world. But for the moment they are intoxicated.
> When they shake off their wine, then they will
> repent."

Jesus explains that he came to us born into flesh. He found them "intoxicated" or filled with lies and misinformation.

Once they find the truth of the spirit, they become sober and then become intoxicated with the knowledge of God and seek to please God.

(29) Jesus said,

> "If the flesh came into being because of spirit, it is a wonder. But if spirit came into being because of the body, it is a wonder of wonders. Indeed, I am amazed at how this great wealth has made its home in this poverty."

Jesus is explaining that human flesh or the body is nothing in comparison to the soul or your light. The body is merely a vehicle providing transportation for your light. It is like saying that a person gets into a car to drive to a location. The car does not get into the body.

(30) Jesus said,

> "Where there are three gods, they are gods. Where there are two or one, I am with him."

Jesus is referring to the Trinity, where there are three gods; they are gods. When the spirit comes together in the light, they are one. Before you gain the knowledge and merge with the all, as the one, Jesus is always with you, guiding you.

(31) Jesus said,

> "No prophet is accepted in his own village; no physician heals those who know him."

Jesus, again using metaphors, is saying that once you gain the knowledge or truth, there are no prophets, as they are pointless.

"No physician heals those who know him," is saying that there are no ills in the light.

(32) Jesus said,

> "A city being built on a high mountain and fortified cannot fall, nor can it be hidden."

A city, or your soul, should be built with the truth of knowledge and fortified. Once you find the truth of God, all can see it, and it cannot be hidden.

(33) Jesus said,

> "Preach from your housetops that which you will hear in your ear. For no one lights a lamp and puts it under a bushel, nor does he put it in a hidden place, but rather he sets it on a lamp stand so that everyone who enters and leaves will see its light."

Once you find the truth, the light, let it shine for all to see.

(34) Jesus said,

> "If a blind man leads a blind man, they will both fall into a pit."

One without the knowledge of the truth cannot lead another, or they will both be doomed.

CHARLES T. ROSS, JR.

(35) Jesus said,

> "It is not possible for anyone to enter the house
> of a strong man and take it by force unless he
> binds his hands; then he will (be able to)
> ransack his house."

Once you find the truth, it cannot be taken from you unless you allow it to happen.

(36) Jesus said,

> "Do not be concerned from morning until
> evening and from evening until morning about
> what you will wear."

Jesus is explaining not to worry or be consumed with the little things in life that don't matter. Focus on the important things like awakening to the knowledge of God and being filled with light.

(37) His disciples said,

> "When will you become revealed to us and
> when shall we see you?"

> Jesus said, "When you disrobe without being
> ashamed and take up your garments and place
> them under your feet like little children and
> tread on them, then will you see the son of the
> living one, and you will not be afraid"

The disciples are asking how to find and recognize Jesus. Jesus explains that once they discover the truth, they will discard their clothing, a metaphor for their humanity, and then they will clearly see God, Jesus, and the kingdom of Heaven.

(38) Jesus said,

> "Many times have you desired to hear these
> words which I am saying to you, and you have
> no one else to hear them from. There will be
> days when you will look for me and will not
> find me."

Who would not like to be in the constant presence of Jesus while living this life? To have him in the flesh, where you could sit and share life with him, would have been an amazing gift. Jesus is referring to telling them of eternal life, the words that they so desperately wanted to hear. He was also foreshadowing his future where he would be crucified and exit the living in flesh state, and they would no longer be able to communicate with him in the same way.

(39) Jesus said,

> "The pharisees and the scribes have taken the
> keys of knowledge (gnosis) and hidden them.
> They themselves have not entered, nor have
> they allowed to enter those who wish to. You,
> however, be as wise as serpents and as
> innocent as doves."

Jesus refers to the truth of the Gospels, referring to the knowledge that the leaders kept hidden from the populace. When those you rule are kept in the dark, they are easier to rule over. Those who know the truth are wise and live life innocently.

(40) Jesus said,

> "A grapevine has been planted outside of the
> father, but being unsound, it will be pulled up
> by its roots and destroyed."

Again, Jesus is speaking in metaphors. The grapevine is the knowledge given to us by God. It is free to all to climb up and reach the top, or the Kingdom of Heaven. Those who seek Heaven without the knowledge will be unable to climb the grapevine and tear it from its roots.

(41) Jesus said,

> "Whoever has something in his hand will
> receive more, and whoever has nothing will be
> deprived of even the little he has."

Those who gain the knowledge will have something to hold onto. Those who have not found the truth have nothing and never will.

(42) Jesus said,

> "Become passers-by."

A passerby is a person who walks past something. Jesus is saying walk past the misdirections and lies. Walk straight to the truth and ignore everything else.

(43) His disciples said to him,

> "Who are you, that you should say these things
> to us?"

"You do not realize who I am from what I say to
you, but you have become like the Jews, for
they (either) love the tree and hate its fruit (or)
love the fruit and hate the tree."

The disciples of Jesus had not yet fully realized who he was.
Jesus is telling them this, saying that they are like the Jews
who hate the one who speaks the truth, but like what he is
saying, or that they hate the truth but like the person speaking
it.

(44) Jesus said,

"Whoever blasphemes against the father will be
forgiven, and whoever blasphemes against the
son will be forgiven, but whoever blasphemes
against the holy spirit will not be forgiven either
on earth or in heaven."

Jesus is proclaiming that you can curse God, you can curse
Jesus, and you will be forgiven. However, if you curse the holy
trinity, or the one, once you become part of it and know the
truth, you will then not be forgiven.

(45) Jesus said,

"Grapes are not harvested from thorns, nor are
figs gathered from thistles, for they do not
produce fruit. A good man brings forth good
from his storehouse; an evil man brings forth
evil things from his evil storehouse, which is in
his heart, and says evil things. For out of the
abundance of the heart he brings forth evil
things."

Jesus is stating that from good comes good, and evil spews forth
evil.

(46) Jesus said,

> "Among those born of women, from Adam until
> John the Baptist, there is no one so superior to
> John the Baptist that his eyes should not be
> lowered (before him). Yet I have said, whichever
> one of you comes to be a child will be
> acquainted with the kingdom and will become
> superior to John."

Jesus says that John the Baptist was a pure soul; he had found God and the truth. No human was purer than he to that point. However, once you find the truth and reach the Kingdom of Heaven, you will then be above John the Baptist or any human.

(47) Jesus said,

> "It is impossible for a man to mount two horses
> or to stretch two bows. And it is impossible for
> a servant to serve two masters; otherwise, he
> will honor the one and treat the other
> contemptuously. No man drinks old wine and
> immediately desires to drink new wine. And
> new wine is not put into old wineskins, lest they
> burst; nor is old wine put into a new wineskin,
> lest it spoil it. An old patch is not sewn onto a
> new garment, because a tear would result."

Jesus is using a metaphor to state that you can not be true to God and a false god at the same time. You must choose the true creator and the truth and concentrate all of yourself into that belief.

(48) Jesus said,

> "If two make peace with each other in this one
> house, they will say to the mountain, 'Move
> Away,' and it will move away."

Again, a metaphor by Jesus stating that you must become one with the body and spirit within you. Once you can do this, no mountain or any other obstacle can stand in your way.

(49) Jesus said,

> "Blessed are the solitary and elect, for you will
> find the kingdom. For you are from it, and to it
> you will return."

Blessed are those who have found and acknowledge the truth. They know that they have come from the Kingdom of Heaven and will once again return to it.

(50) Jesus said,

> "If they say to you, 'Where did you come
> from?', say to them, 'We came from the light,
> the place where the light came into being on its
> own accord and established itself and became
> manifest through their image.' If they say to
> you, 'Is it you?', say, 'We are its children, we are
> the elect of the living father.' If they ask you,
> 'What is the sign of your father in you?', say to
> them, 'It is movement and repose.'"

Jesus is acknowledging the light that is the sole. The light that is God. We came from the light, we are light. Living as humans, we are the chosen ones of God to experience this for him.

(51) His disciples said to him,

"When will the repose of the dead come about,
and when will the new world come?"

He said to them, "What you look forward to has
already come, but you do not recognize it."

Jesus was asked when the dead would rise, and we would see the new world. Jesus states that it already is. We have all already died and lived. The soul or light is immortal.

Because you have not found the truth, you cannot see it, but it is right here staring at you.

(52) His disciples said to him,

"Twenty-four prophets spoke in Israel, and all of
them spoke in you."

He said to them, "You have omitted the one
living in your presence and have spoken (only)
of the dead."

The disciples are speaking to Jesus about the previous prophets whose words had been written. Jesus is telling them that they are ignoring the most important prophet of them all. The one sitting and talking to them, Christ himself.

(53) His disciples said to him,

"Is circumcision beneficial or not?"

He said to them, "If it were beneficial, their
father would beget them already circumcised
from their mother. Rather, the true circumcision
in spirit has become completely profitable."

Jesus was asked if it was beneficial, religiously speaking, to be circumcised or not. Obviously referring to the Old Testament, where Abraham seals a covenant with God by circumcision. Jesus says that if circumcision were needed, we would have been born like that. The true spirit of the covenant is within you and not a mark of the human body.

(54) Jesus said,

> "Blessed are the poor, for yours is the kingdom
> of heaven."

Money, wealth, personal possessions, etc., are all useless. You take nothing with you passing into the Kingdom of Heaven, but gain everything once there.

(55) Jesus said,

> "Whoever does not hate his father and his
> mother cannot become a disciple to me. And
> whoever does not hate his brothers and sisters
> and take up his cross in my way will not be
> worthy of me."

Jesus is not saying that you must hate all other people. He is stating that you must place Jesus and God above all others to be a follower of his.

(56) Jesus said,

> "Whoever has come to understand the world
> has found (only) a corpse, and whoever has
> found a corpse is superior to the world."

One who has discovered the truth knows that the human body
is merely a temporary vessel to gain knowledge and experience.
A corpse, or a dead person, has returned to the Kingdom of
Heaven and is far superior to the living world.

(57) Jesus said,

> "The kingdom of the father is like a man who
> had good seed. His enemy came by night and
> sowed weeds among the good seed. The man
> did not allow them to pull up the weeds; he
> said to them, 'I am afraid that you will go
> intending to pull up the weeds and pull up the
> wheat along with them.' For on the day of the
> harvest the weeds will be plainly visible, and
> they will be pulled up and burned."

Jesus is saying that the non-believers, those who have failed to
unveil the truth, will stand out like weeds, and those weeds will
be pulled from the field.

(58) Jesus said,

> "Blessed is the man who has suffered and
> found life."

Blessed is the one who finds the truth and lives from there.

(59) Jesus said,

> "Take heed of the living one while you are alive,
> lest you die and seek to see him and be unable
> to do so."

Jesus is saying Take note of me here on Earth and learn from me
and behold me so that you can find me in Heaven. If you can't
find me here on Earth, you won't have the opportunity to do so
in Heaven.

(60)

> A Samaritan carrying a lamb on his way to
> Judea.

He said to his disciples, "That man is round
about the lamb."

> They said to him, "So that he may kill it and
> eat it."

He said to them, "While it is alive, he will not
eat it, but only when he has killed it and it has
become a corpse."

> They said to him, "He cannot do so otherwise."

He said to them, "You too, look for a place for
yourself within repose, lest you become a
corpse and be eaten."

Jesus is saying to his disciples that they are seeking Heaven on
Earth, but will not find it until they have died and have returned
to God in the Kingdom of Heaven.

(61) Jesus said,

"Two will rest on a bed: the one will die, and the
other will live."

> Salome said, "Who are you, man, that you ...
> have come up on my couch and eaten from my
> table?"

Jesus said to her, "I am he who exists from the
undivided. I was given some of the things of my
father." <...> "I am your disciple." <...>
"Therefore I say, if he is destroyed, he will be
filled with light, but if he is divided, he will be
filled with darkness."

Jesus states to Salome that he exists from the "Undivided" God. "I was given some of the things of my father" Jesus was born with his spiritual memory. Jesus states that one who dies with the knowledge is filled with light. However, if he remains divided from the light, knowledge is unattained. He will then remain divided, separate from the light, thus filled with darkness.

(62) Jesus said,

"It is to those who are worthy of my mysteries
that I tell my mysteries. Do not let your left
(hand) know what your right (hand) is doing."

Jesus is using metaphors and is referring to the body and spirit as being hands. Don't let your body know what your spirit is doing, which is seeking the truth. You don't want your body or doubts to lead the way and lead you down the wrong path.

(63) Jesus said,

"There was a rich man who had much money. He said, 'I shall put my money to use so that I may sow, reap, plant, and fill my storehouse with produce, with the result that I shall lack nothing.' Such were his intentions, but that same night he died. Let him who has ears hear."

Jesus is saying that all of the money and material possessions that you can achieve in life mean nothing once you have died. The "rich" man died, never finding the light, so he, in fact, lacked everything.

(64) Jesus said,

"A man had received visitors. And when he had prepared the dinner, he sent his servant to invite the guests. He went to the first one and said to him, 'My master invites you.' He said, 'I have claims against some merchants. They are coming to me this evening. I must go and give them my orders. I ask to be excused from the dinner.' He went to another and said to him, 'My master has invited you.' He said to him, 'I have just bought a house and am required for the day. I shall not have any spare time.' He went to another and said to him, 'My master invites you.' He said to him, 'My friend is going to get married, and I am to prepare the banquet. I shall not be able to come. I ask to be excused from the dinner.'

> He went to another and said to him, 'My master invites you.' He said to him, 'I have just bought a farm, and I am on my way to collect the rent. I shall not be able to come. I ask to be excused.' The servant returned and said to his master, 'Those whom you invited to the dinner have asked to be excused.' The master said to his servant, 'Go outside to the streets and bring back those whom you happen to meet, so that they may dine.' Businessmen and merchants will not enter the places of my father."

Jesus, again using metaphors, is speaking as God, inviting those who have wealth and have achieved much in life to join him. Those asked found nothing better than excuses to continue gathering wealth, luxury, and delaying the inevitable of joining God. Jesus then says that those who are not seeking excuses, or in other words, not pursuing useless tasks, will find him and join him.

(65) He said,

> "There was a good man who owned a vineyard. He leased it to tenant farmers so that they might work it and he might collect the produce from them. He sent his servant so that the tenants might give him the produce of the vineyard. They seized his servant and beat him, all but killing him. The servant went back and told his master. The master said, 'Perhaps he did not recognize them.' He sent another servant. The tenants beat this one as well. Then the owner sent his son and said, 'Perhaps they will show respect to my son.' Because the tenants knew that it was he who was the heir to the vineyard, they seized him and killed him. Let him who has ears hear."

Here, Jesus uses a mighty metaphor. God is the good man who owns the vineyard. The vineyard is the Earth. The tenants are people. God's servants that he sent to the tenants were prophets. God then sent his son, Jesus, who they crucified.

(66) Jesus said,

> "Show me the stone which the builders have rejected. That one is the cornerstone."

In this metaphor, the builders are the religious leaders. Jesus is the cornerstone.

(67) Jesus said,

> "If one who knows the all still feels a personal deficiency, he is completely deficient."

One cannot find the truth and be deficient in any way. If one thinks he has found the all, or the truth, but still thinks that he is deficient, he has not found the truth.

(68) Jesus said,

> "Blessed are you when you are hated and persecuted. Wherever you have been persecuted they will find no place."

The ones who have found the truth and are one with God will be hated and persecuted by non-believers. Those who persecute you will not find the truth and have no place in the light.

(69) Jesus said,

> "Blessed are they who have been persecuted
> within themselves. It is they who have truly
> come to know the father. Blessed are the
> hungry, for the belly of him who desires will be
> filled."

Blessed are the people who have battled the misbeliefs and doubts within themselves and have, through it all, found the truth. Those who are hungry for knowledge will find it and be fully satisfied in every way.

(70) Jesus said,

> "That which you have will save you if you bring
> it forth from yourselves. That which you do not
> have within you will kill you if you do not have it
> within you."

"That which you have", your light or soul, will save you if you bring it forth from within yourself. If you don't have it within you to bring forth your light, the lack of knowledge will kill you.

(71) Jesus said,

> "I shall destroy this house, and no one will be
> able to build it [...]."

Jesus is referring to either the human body or the Earth as being 'this house'. No one other than God could destroy this house.

(72) A man said to him,

"Tell my brothers to divide my father's
possessions with me."

He said to him, "O man, who has made me a
divider?" He turned to his disciples and said to
them, "I am not a divider, am I?"

God sent his son, Jesus, to Earth to teach and deliver the truth. He did not send Jesus to judge mankind; he sent him to save us. When Jesus died on the cross for our sins, he didn't do it for some; he did it for all.

(73) Jesus said,

"The harvest is great but the laborers are few.
Beseech the Lord, therefore, to send out
laborers to the harvest."

Once you find the truth of God, the "harvest", there is no better reward. Jesus is saying that there are few who are seeking the truth.

(74) He said,

"O Lord, there are many around the drinking
trough, but there is nothing in the cistern."

Jesus is telling God that many are seeking truth but are finding no one to tell it to them.

(75) Jesus said,

> "Many are standing at the door, but it is the
> solitary who will enter the bridal chamber."

Jesus is stating that many are wanting to enter the gateway or door to the Kingdom of Heaven, but it is the one who will gain entry. In other words, all goes back to the One, and becoming part of it by finding the truth.

(76) Jesus said,

> "The kingdom of the father is like a merchant
> who had a consignment of merchandise and
> who discovered a pearl. That merchant was
> shrewd.
>
> He sold the merchandise and bought the pearl
> alone for himself. You too, seek his unfailing
> and enduring treasure where no moth comes
> near to devour and no worm destroys."

You can look at this metaphor as the oyster that contains the pearl as the human body, and the pearl as your soul, the light. The treasure is the pearl, the soul when it leaves the body and returns to Heaven, where it has eternity and cannot be destroyed.

(77) Jesus said,

> "It is I who am the light which is above them all.
> It is I who am the all. From me did the all come
> forth, and unto me did the all extend. Split a
> piece of wood, and I am there. Lift up the
> stone, and you will find me there."

God is the true light and creator of all. God is part of everything, everything is part of God, making the ALL.

(78) Jesus said,

> "Why have you come out into the desert? To see a reed shaken by the wind? And to see a man clothed in fine garments like your kings and your great men? Upon them are the fine garments, and they are unable to discern the truth."

Jesus is saying, Seek solitude to find the truth of light within yourself. Even Kings and the rich cannot find the truth.

(79)

> A woman from the crowd said to him, "Blessed are the womb which bore you and the breasts which nourished you."

> He said to her, "Blessed are those who have heard the word of the father and have truly kept it. For there will be days when you will say, 'Blessed are the womb which has not conceived and the breasts which have not given milk.'"

An anonymous woman in the crowd told Jesus, "Blessed are the womb which bore you and the breast which nourished you." Jesus replied that the blessed ones are those who have heard and followed the word of God. Jesus then refers to returning to the spirit, where there are no wombs to carry children or breasts to nourish them.

(80) Jesus said,

> "He who has recognized the world has found
> the body, but he who has found the body is
> superior to the world."

Jesus again refers to the soul. Your soul within your body has recognized the body, finding the truth, and is therefore superior to the world.

(81) Jesus said,

> "Let him who has grown rich be king, and let
> him who possesses power renounce it."

Jesus is saying that there is no glory in becoming rich, being the king, or possessing power.

(82) Jesus said,

> "He who is near me is near the fire, and he who
> is far from me is far from the kingdom."

The fire is the light of God. If you are not near Jesus, you are far from God and the Kingdom of Heaven.

(83) Jesus said,

> "The images are manifest to man, but the light
> in them remains concealed in the image of the
> light of the father. He will become manifest, but
> his image will remain concealed by his light."

God has instilled the light, your soul within your human body. That light will remain hidden from you until you find the truth.

Even once you have found the light, you will find that the true image of God is light itself.

(84) Jesus said,

> "When you see your likeness, you rejoice. But when you see your images which came into being before you, and which neither die not become manifest, how much you will have to bear!"

Jesus is referring to your true self as being eternal light. Your light or soul has no death; it is eternal. That knowledge, when you finally find it, is overwhelming.

(85) Jesus said,

> "Adam came into being from a great power and a great wealth, but he did not become worthy of you. For had he been worthy, he would not have experienced death."

God gave humanity life in the Garden of Eden, beginning with Adam. Because Adam and Eve did not obey God's rules set forth, they were banished from the garden where they could have lived and thrived forever.

(86) Jesus said,

> "The foxes have their holes and the birds have their nests, but the son of man has no place to lay his head and rest."

The foxes, birds, and other animals have their homes. Our true home is the Kingdom of Heaven. You will never truly be at rest until you have returned to the Kingdom.

(87) Jesus said,

> "Wretched is the body that is dependant upon
> a body, and wretched is the soul that is
> dependent on these two."

Wretched is the soul that is wholly dependent upon the human body. Wretched is the soul that is dependent upon the soul and the body.

(88) Jesus said,

> "The angels and the prophets will come to you
> and give to you those things you (already) have.
> And you too, give them those things which you
> have, and say to yourselves, 'When will they
> come and take what is theirs?'"

The Angels will come to you and give you the knowledge of the light, which you already possess and ignore. You then ask when will they take my soul and return it to the Kingdom.

(89) Jesus said,

> "Why do you wash the outside of the cup? Do
> you not realize that he who made the inside is
> the same one who made the outside?"

Jesus refers to the human body as a cup. In other words, why do you pay so much attention to the body and not the soul?

(90) Jesus said,

> "Come unto me, for my yoke is easy and my
> lordship is mild, and you will find repose for
> yourselves."

Jesus states, Come to me, you will find peace and love.

(91) They said to him,

> "Tell us who you are so that we may believe in
> you." He said to them, "You read the face of the
> sky and of the earth, but you have not
> recognized the one who is before you, and you
> do not know how to read this moment."

Jesus is stating that he is God, and because they don't know
God, they are unable to recognize what/who they are seeing.

(92) Jesus said,

> "Seek and you will find. Yet, what you asked
> me about in former times and which I did not
> tell you then, now I do desire to tell, but you do
> not inquire after it."

Jesus is asking for them to repeat what they once asked him
about and no longer do. He is stating that when asked prior, he
did not feel that they were ready to hear. Now that they are
ready to hear, they are fearing the answer that he may give.

(93)

> "Do not give what is holy to dogs, lest they
> throw them on the dungheap. Do not throw the
> pearls to swine, lest they [...] it [...]."

Jesus is using dogs as a metaphor for nonbelievers. Don't give what is holy to those who are not holy. Don't give the intelligence to those who will throw it away.

(94) Jesus said,

> "He who seeks will find, and he who knocks will
> be let in."

Seek the light, the truth, and you will find it. The truth will bring you to the door of the Kingdom of Heaven. If you can find the door, a simple knock will grant you entrance.

(95) Jesus said,

> "If you have money, do not lend it at interest,
> but give it to one from whom you will not get it
> back."

Jesus is saying Be kind. If you have more than you need, be willing to give it to others who need it, not expecting anything in return. Life is not about greed or obtaining all material things before you die.

(96) Jesus said,

> "The kingdom of the father is like a certain
> woman. She took a little leaven, concealed it in
> some dough, and made it into large loaves. Let
> him who has ears hear."

God created the Heavens from nothing and has grown it into a
bountiful harvest for all.

(97) Jesus said,

> "The kingdom of the father is like a certain
> woman who was carrying a jar full of meal.
> While she was walking on the road, still some
> distance from home, the handle of the jar broke
> and the meal emptied out behind her on the
> road. She did not realize it; she had noticed no
> accident. When she reached her house, she set
> the jar down and found it empty."

Jesus is using another metaphor. Meal refers to the knowledge
of the truth. God is the woman carrying the jar of knowledge.
The jar was spilt out upon the Earth, and it was not by accident.

(98) Jesus said,

> "The kingdom of the father is like a certain man
> who wanted to kill a powerful man. In his own
> house he drew his sword and stuck it into the
> wall in order to find out whether his hand could
> carry through. Then he slew the powerful man."

The Kingdom of the Father is Heaven. In Heaven, a 'powerful man" is nothing. No man gets into Heaven, so that a man is slain before ever entering into Heaven. Only souls enter Heaven, not bodies or a man. No strength or power gained as a man has any bearing on Heaven.

(99) The disciples said to him,

> "Your brothers and your mother are standing outside."

> He said to them, "Those here who do the will of my father are my brothers and my mother. It is they who will enter the kingdom of my father."

Jesus is referring to all of humanity being his family. All that do the will of their Father, God, will find Heaven.

(100)

> They showed Jesus a gold coin and said to him, "Caesar's men demand taxes from us." He said to them, "Give Caesar what belongs to Caesar, give God what belongs to God, and give me what is mine."

Jesus tells his disciples that God is not concerned with money or other Earthly material items. God wants your love and for you to find the truth. What belongs to God is you, your soul. Give to God what is his, your soul. Give to Jesus love and respect, for he is God's only son.

(101)

> "Whoever does not hate his father and his
> mother as I do cannot become a disciple to me.
> And whoever does not love his father and his
> mother as I do cannot become a disciple to me.
> For my mother [...], but my true mother gave
> me life."

You must love God above all else. You must love all others. If you are unable to do that, you are not able to be a disciple of Jesus. God gave life to all, including Jesus, for he is Father, Mother to all.

(102) Jesus said,

> "Woe to the pharisees, for they are like a dog
> sleeping in the manger of oxen, for neither does
> he eat nor does he let the oxen eat."

Jesus is stating that the Pharaohs reject the knowledge of God, the truth. They, in turn, do not allow their subjects to accept the truth of God.

(103) Jesus said,

> "Fortunate is the man who knows where the
> brigands will enter, so that he may get up,
> muster his domain, and arm himself before they
> invade."

A brigand is a thief. Arm yourself with the knowledge of the truth. Once you have done that, no one can take it from you. You will see false hoods, misdirection, lies, and other attempts to control you so that they cannot harm you.

(104) They said to Jesus,

"Come, let us pray today and let us fast."

Jesus said, "What is the sin that I have
committed, or wherein have I been defeated?
But when the bridegroom leaves the bridal
chamber, then let them fast and pray."

When asked to pray and fast with his disciples, Jesus says that
the time to pray and fast for forgiveness is when I have left you.
In other words, when and if they decide to leave him/God.

(105) Jesus said,

"He who knows the father and the mother will
be called the son of a harlot."

Jesus refers to the nonbelievers, stating that one who knows the
truth of God will be called liars.

(106) Jesus said,

"When you make the two one, you will become
the sons of man, and when you say, 'Mountain,
move away,' it will move away."

The "two" are the body and soul. When you find the truth and
merge them as one, all is possible. You will realize that
mountains, and everything else, is just a facade, a matrix,
whatever you want to think of it as. It is merely a projection
from God. Once you become part of God, those simple things
like mountains become nothing.

(107) Jesus said,

> "The kingdom is like a shepherd who had a hundred sheep. One of them, the largest, went astray. He left the ninety-nine sheep and looked for that one until he found it. When he had gone to such trouble, he said to the sheep, 'I care for you more than the ninety-nine.'"

Jesus is stating that God deeply cares and loves us all. When one is led astray, he will seek out that soul and try to bring them back to the "flock' because that is how much he loves us all.

It's not that he doesn't care about the 99 that didn't leave. For they had already found him, and another needed his attention more at that moment.

(108) Jesus said,

> "He who will drink from my mouth will become like me. I myself shall become he, and the things that are hidden will be revealed to him."

He who listens to Jesus, seeks to understand his words, will have the knowledge of truth revealed to him. He will become me, and I will become him because we are all part of the ONE. NO truth is revealed from anyone who finds the truth.

(109) Jesus said,

"The kingdom is like a man who had a hidden treasure in his field without knowing it. And after he died, he left it to his son. The son did not know (about the treasure).

He inherited the field and sold it. And the one who bought it went plowing and found the treasure. He began to lend money at interest to whomever he wished."

The truth of God is like a treasure. In this metaphor, a man died having never discovered the truth during his life; therefore, he could not leave the unfound knowledge to his son, even though it had been in plain sight all of the time. The son was also unable to find the truth hidden in plain sight. The other man found the truth and shared it with all he desired and profited from it.

(110) Jesus said,

"Whoever finds the world and becomes rich, let him renounce the world."

Whoever finds the truth of God will gain possession of all and can renounce the world, for it means nothing in the light of God.

(111) Jesus said,

"The heavens and the earth will be rolled up in your presence. And the one who lives from the living one will not see death." Does not Jesus say, "Whoever finds himself is superior to the world?"

Again, Jesus refers to finding the truth, the light, the knowledge of God, as finding eternity. When you realize you are a part of the One, you realize that you are indeed far too superior to the world or any other material object.

(112) Jesus said,

> "Woe to the flesh that depends on the soul;
> woe to the soul that depends on the flesh."

Shame on the person whose ignorance causes the two (body and soul) to be dependent upon one another. Live as the ONE that you are.

(113) His disciples said to him,

> "When will the kingdom come?" "It will not come by waiting for it.
>
> It will not be a matter of saying 'here it is' or 'there it is.' Rather, the kingdom of the father is spread out upon the earth, and men do not see it."

The disciples asked Jesus when the Kingdom of Heaven would come. Jesus replied, saying that they are already in the Kingdom of Heaven. They just don't realize it. Everything is Heaven, Everything is God. We are part of God. God is part of us. The ONE.

(114) Simon Peter said to him,

> "Let Mary leave us, for women are not worthy of life."

> Jesus said, "I myself shall lead her in order to make her male, so that she too may become a living spirit resembling you males. For every woman who will make herself male will enter the kingdom of heaven."

This is another metaphor of Jesus. Being "male' or 'female" refers to the soul. The soul is not one gender or the other. Becoming male refers to finding the truth and realizing that we are all one. Once you realize you are ONE, you will enter the Kingdom of Heaven.

⟿

THE GOSPEL ACCORDING TO
THOMAS

⌘

*T*he above Gospel was Christ himself explaining the path of enlightenment to all. You will have noticed how Christ never spoke of Hell, Satan, or a second coming. Christ already bestowed the presence of God upon us with life among us. He died for our sins and granted all of us eternal paradise. Why would he need to come back a second time? Coming back a second time would mean that what he did the first time was flawed. God does NOT make mistakes. The Holy Bible and Revelations within it are also written in metaphors. Try looking at the seven seals mentioned as the seven chakras in the human body. As each 'seal' is broken, more revelations are made. In fact, 144,000 of them.

I wrote this short book to introduce all to these simple concepts. I will be writing a series of books, with each book being dedicated to a single topic. These books will take an in-depth look at complex topics. The goal is to show all what a wonderful universe we live in and the constant connection to God that we all have.

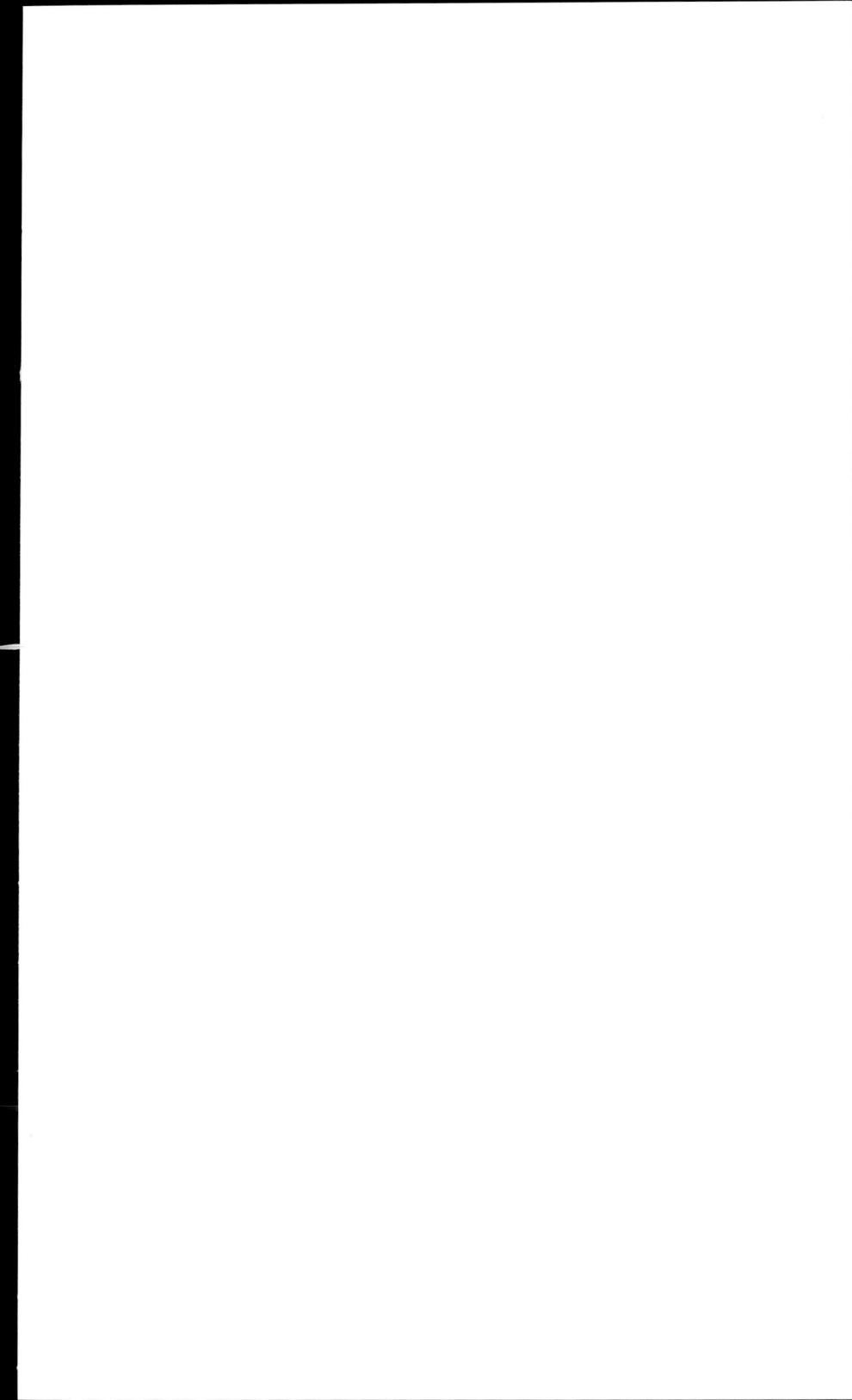

www.ingramcontent.com/pod-product-compliance
Lightning Source LLC
Chambersburg PA
CBHW061457040426
42450CB00008B/1388